This gymnastic scorebook belongs to:

If you have time, please leave an online review. It means the world to us!

For questions, Requests and suggestions about this book, Please don't hesitate to contact us at: logjournals@gmail.com

Thank You so Much!

📅 DATE	📍 M█████

GYMNASTIC LEVEL	

	PERSONAL BEST	TODAY'S SCORE
BEAM		
FLOOR		
BARS		
VAULT		
ALL AROUND		

GOALS: _____

_____

_____

_____

_____

FLOOR ROUTINE

I DID WELL	MUST WORK ON

BEAM

I DID WELL	MUST WORK ON

VAULT

I DID WELL	MUST WORK ON

BARS

I DID WELL	MUST WORK ON

📅 DATE	📍 MEET LOCATION

GYMNASTIC LEVEL	

	PERSONAL BEST	TODAY'S SCORE
BEAM		
FLOOR		
BARS		
VAULT		
ALL AROUND		

GOALS: _____

_____

_____

_____

_____

FLOOR ROUTINE

I DID WELL	MUST WORK ON

BEAM

I DID WELL	MUST WORK ON

VAULT

I DID WELL	MUST WORK ON

BARS

I DID WELL	MUST WORK ON

📅 DATE	📍 MEET LOCATION

GYMNASTIC LEVEL	

	PERSONAL BEST	TODAY'S SCORE
BEAM		
FLOOR		
BARS		
VAULT		
ALL AROUND		

GOALS: _____
_____
_____
_____
_____
_____

FLOOR ROUTINE	
I DID WELL	MUST WORK ON

BEAM	
I DID WELL	MUST WORK ON

VAULT	
I DID WELL	MUST WORK ON

BARS	
I DID WELL	MUST WORK ON

📅 DATE	📍 MEET LOCATION

GYMNASTIC LEVEL	

	PERSONAL BEST	TODAY'S SCORE
BEAM		
FLOOR		
BARS		
VAULT		
ALL AROUND		

GOALS: _____

_____

_____

_____

_____

_____

FLOOR ROUTINE

I DID WELL	MUST WORK ON

BEAM

I DID WELL	MUST WORK ON

VAULT

I DID WELL	MUST WORK ON

BARS

I DID WELL	MUST WORK ON

📅 DATE	📍 MEET LOCATION

GYMNASTIC LEVEL	

	PERSONAL BEST	TODAY'S SCORE
BEAM		
FLOOR		
BARS		
VAULT		
ALL AROUND		

GOALS: _____
_____
_____
_____
_____
_____

FLOOR ROUTINE

I DID WELL	MUST WORK ON

BEAM

I DID WELL	MUST WORK ON

VAULT

I DID WELL	MUST WORK ON

BARS

I DID WELL	MUST WORK ON

📅 DATE	📍 MEET LOCATION

GYMNASTIC LEVEL	

	PERSONAL BEST	TODAY'S SCORE
BEAM		
FLOOR		
BARS		
VAULT		
ALL AROUND		

GOALS: _____
_____
_____
_____
_____
_____

FLOOR ROUTINE	
I DID WELL	MUST WORK ON

BEAM	
I DID WELL	MUST WORK ON

VAULT	
I DID WELL	MUST WORK ON

BARS	
I DID WELL	MUST WORK ON

📅 DATE	📍 MEET LOCATION

GYMNASTIC LEVEL	

	PERSONAL BEST	TODAY'S SCORE
BEAM		
FLOOR		
BARS		
VAULT		
ALL AROUND		

GOALS: _____

_____

_____

_____

_____

FLOOR ROUTINE	
I DID WELL	MUST WORK ON

BEAM	
I DID WELL	MUST WORK ON

VAULT	
I DID WELL	MUST WORK ON

BARS	
I DID WELL	MUST WORK ON

📅 DATE	📍 MEET LOCATION

GYMNASTIC LEVEL	

	PERSONAL BEST	TODAY'S SCORE
BEAM		
FLOOR		
BARS		
VAULT		
ALL AROUND		

GOALS: _____
_____
_____
_____
_____
_____

FLOOR ROUTINE

I DID WELL	MUST WORK ON

BEAM

I DID WELL	MUST WORK ON

VAULT

I DID WELL	MUST WORK ON

BARS

I DID WELL	MUST WORK ON

📅 DATE	📍 MEET LOCATION

GYMNASTIC LEVEL	

	PERSONAL BEST	TODAY'S SCORE
BEAM		
FLOOR		
BARS		
VAULT		
ALL AROUND		

GOALS: _____

_____

_____

_____

_____

FLOOR ROUTINE

I DID WELL	MUST WORK ON

BEAM

I DID WELL	MUST WORK ON

VAULT

I DID WELL	MUST WORK ON

BARS

I DID WELL	MUST WORK ON

📅 DATE	📍 MEET LOCATION

GYMNASTIC LEVEL	

	PERSONAL BEST	TODAY'S SCORE
BEAM		
FLOOR		
BARS		
VAULT		
ALL AROUND		

GOALS: _____

_____

_____

_____

_____

FLOOR ROUTINE

I DID WELL	MUST WORK ON

BEAM

I DID WELL	MUST WORK ON

VAULT

I DID WELL	MUST WORK ON

BARS

I DID WELL	MUST WORK ON

📅 DATE	📍 MEET LOCATION

GYMNASTIC LEVEL	

	PERSONAL BEST	TODAY'S SCORE
BEAM		
FLOOR		
BARS		
VAULT		
ALL AROUND		

GOALS: _____
_____
_____
_____
_____

FLOOR ROUTINE

I DID WELL	MUST WORK ON

BEAM

I DID WELL	MUST WORK ON

VAULT

I DID WELL	MUST WORK ON

BARS

I DID WELL	MUST WORK ON

📅 DATE	📍 MEET LOCATION

GYMNASTIC LEVEL	

	PERSONAL BEST	TODAY'S SCORE
BEAM		
FLOOR		
BARS		
VAULT		
ALL AROUND		

GOALS: _____
_____
_____
_____
_____

FLOOR ROUTINE	
I DID WELL	MUST WORK ON

BEAM	
I DID WELL	MUST WORK ON

VAULT	
I DID WELL	MUST WORK ON

BARS	
I DID WELL	MUST WORK ON

📅 DATE	📍 MEET LOCATION

GYMNASTIC LEVEL	

	PERSONAL BEST	TODAY'S SCORE
BEAM		
FLOOR		
BARS		
VAULT		
ALL AROUND		

GOALS: _____

_____

_____

_____

_____

FLOOR ROUTINE

I DID WELL	MUST WORK ON

BEAM

I DID WELL	MUST WORK ON

VAULT

I DID WELL	MUST WORK ON

BARS

I DID WELL	MUST WORK ON

📅 DATE	📍 MEET LOCATION

GYMNASTIC LEVEL	

	PERSONAL BEST	TODAY'S SCORE
BEAM		
FLOOR		
BARS		
VAULT		
ALL AROUND		

GOALS: _____
_____
_____
_____
_____

FLOOR ROUTINE

I DID WELL	MUST WORK ON

BEAM

I DID WELL	MUST WORK ON

VAULT

I DID WELL	MUST WORK ON

BARS

I DID WELL	MUST WORK ON

📅 DATE	📍 MEET LOCATION

GYMNASTIC LEVEL	

	PERSONAL BEST	TODAY'S SCORE
BEAM		
FLOOR		
BARS		
VAULT		
ALL AROUND		

GOALS: _____

_____

_____

_____

_____

FLOOR ROUTINE

I DID WELL	MUST WORK ON

BEAM

I DID WELL	MUST WORK ON

VAULT

I DID WELL	MUST WORK ON

BARS

I DID WELL	MUST WORK ON

📅 DATE	📍 MEET LOCATION

GYMNASTIC LEVEL	

	PERSONAL BEST	TODAY'S SCORE
BEAM		
FLOOR		
BARS		
VAULT		
ALL AROUND		

GOALS: _____
_____
_____
_____
_____
_____

FLOOR ROUTINE	
I DID WELL	MUST WORK ON

BEAM	
I DID WELL	MUST WORK ON

VAULT	
I DID WELL	MUST WORK ON

BARS	
I DID WELL	MUST WORK ON

📅 DATE	📍 MEET LOCATION

GYMNASTIC LEVEL	

	PERSONAL BEST	TODAY'S SCORE
BEAM		
FLOOR		
BARS		
VAULT		
ALL AROUND		

GOALS: _____

_____

_____

_____

_____

FLOOR ROUTINE

I DID WELL	MUST WORK ON

BEAM

I DID WELL	MUST WORK ON

VAULT

I DID WELL	MUST WORK ON

BARS

I DID WELL	MUST WORK ON

📅 DATE	📍 MEET LOCATION

GYMNASTIC LEVEL	

	PERSONAL BEST	TODAY'S SCORE
BEAM		
FLOOR		
BARS		
VAULT		
ALL AROUND		

GOALS: _____

_____

_____

_____

_____

FLOOR ROUTINE	
I DID WELL	MUST WORK ON

BEAM	
I DID WELL	MUST WORK ON

VAULT	
I DID WELL	MUST WORK ON

BARS	
I DID WELL	MUST WORK ON

📅 DATE	📍 MEET LOCATION

GYMNASTIC LEVEL	

	PERSONAL BEST	TODAY'S SCORE
BEAM		
FLOOR		
BARS		
VAULT		
ALL AROUND		

GOALS: _____

_____

_____

_____

_____

FLOOR ROUTINE	
I DID WELL	MUST WORK ON

BEAM	
I DID WELL	MUST WORK ON

VAULT	
I DID WELL	MUST WORK ON

BARS	
I DID WELL	MUST WORK ON

📅 DATE	📍 MEET LOCATION

GYMNASTIC LEVEL	

	PERSONAL BEST	TODAY'S SCORE
BEAM		
FLOOR		
BARS		
VAULT		
ALL AROUND		

GOALS: _____
_____
_____
_____
_____

FLOOR ROUTINE	
I DID WELL	MUST WORK ON

BEAM	
I DID WELL	MUST WORK ON

VAULT	
I DID WELL	MUST WORK ON

BARS	
I DID WELL	MUST WORK ON

📅 DATE	📍 MEET LOCATION

GYMNASTIC LEVEL	

	PERSONAL BEST	TODAY'S SCORE
BEAM		
FLOOR		
BARS		
VAULT		
ALL AROUND		

GOALS: _____

_____

_____

_____

_____

FLOOR ROUTINE

I DID WELL	MUST WORK ON

BEAM

I DID WELL	MUST WORK ON

VAULT

I DID WELL	MUST WORK ON

BARS

I DID WELL	MUST WORK ON

📅 DATE	📍 MEET LOCATION

GYMNASTIC LEVEL	

	PERSONAL BEST	TODAY'S SCORE
BEAM		
FLOOR		
BARS		
VAULT		
ALL AROUND		

GOALS: _____

_____

_____

_____

_____

FLOOR ROUTINE	
I DID WELL	MUST WORK ON

BEAM	
I DID WELL	MUST WORK ON

VAULT	
I DID WELL	MUST WORK ON

BARS	
I DID WELL	MUST WORK ON

	DATE	MEET LOCATION

GYMNASTIC LEVEL	

	PERSONAL BEST	TODAY'S SCORE
BEAM		
FLOOR		
BARS		
VAULT		
ALL AROUND		

GOALS: _____

_____

_____

_____

_____

FLOOR ROUTINE

I DID WELL	MUST WORK ON

BEAM

I DID WELL	MUST WORK ON

VAULT

I DID WELL	MUST WORK ON

BARS

I DID WELL	MUST WORK ON

📅 DATE	📍 MEET LOCATION

GYMNASTIC LEVEL	

	PERSONAL BEST	TODAY'S SCORE
BEAM		
FLOOR		
BARS		
VAULT		
ALL AROUND		

GOALS: _____
_____
_____
_____
_____
_____

FLOOR ROUTINE	
I DID WELL	MUST WORK ON

BEAM	
I DID WELL	MUST WORK ON

VAULT	
I DID WELL	MUST WORK ON

BARS	
I DID WELL	MUST WORK ON

📅 DATE	📍 MEET LOCATION

GYMNASTIC LEVEL	

	PERSONAL BEST	TODAY'S SCORE
BEAM		
FLOOR		
BARS		
VAULT		
ALL AROUND		

GOALS: _____
_____
_____
_____
_____

FLOOR ROUTINE	
I DID WELL	MUST WORK ON

BEAM	
I DID WELL	MUST WORK ON

VAULT	
I DID WELL	MUST WORK ON

BARS	
I DID WELL	MUST WORK ON

📅 DATE	📍 MEET LOCATION

GYMNASTIC LEVEL	

	PERSONAL BEST	TODAY'S SCORE
BEAM		
FLOOR		
BARS		
VAULT		
ALL AROUND		

GOALS: _____
_____
_____
_____
_____
_____

FLOOR ROUTINE

I DID WELL	MUST WORK ON

BEAM

I DID WELL	MUST WORK ON

VAULT

I DID WELL	MUST WORK ON

BARS

I DID WELL	MUST WORK ON

📅 DATE	📍 MEET LOCATION

GYMNASTIC LEVEL	

	PERSONAL BEST	TODAY'S SCORE
BEAM		
FLOOR		
BARS		
VAULT		
ALL AROUND		

GOALS: _____

_____

_____

_____

_____

FLOOR ROUTINE

I DID WELL	MUST WORK ON

BEAM

I DID WELL	MUST WORK ON

VAULT

I DID WELL	MUST WORK ON

BARS

I DID WELL	MUST WORK ON

🗓 DATE	📍 MEET LOCATION

GYMNASTIC LEVEL	

	PERSONAL BEST	TODAY'S SCORE
BEAM		
FLOOR		
BARS		
VAULT		
ALL AROUND		

GOALS: _____
_____
_____
_____
_____
_____

FLOOR ROUTINE	
I DID WELL	MUST WORK ON

BEAM	
I DID WELL	MUST WORK ON

VAULT	
I DID WELL	MUST WORK ON

BARS	
I DID WELL	MUST WORK ON

🗓 DATE	📍 MEET LOCATION

GYMNASTIC LEVEL	

	PERSONAL BEST	TODAY'S SCORE
BEAM		
FLOOR		
BARS		
VAULT		
ALL AROUND		

GOALS: _____
_____
_____
_____
_____
_____

FLOOR ROUTINE	
I DID WELL	MUST WORK ON

BEAM	
I DID WELL	MUST WORK ON

VAULT	
I DID WELL	MUST WORK ON

BARS	
I DID WELL	MUST WORK ON

📅 DATE	📍 MEET LOCATION

GYMNASTIC LEVEL	

	PERSONAL BEST	TODAY'S SCORE
BEAM		
FLOOR		
BARS		
VAULT		
ALL AROUND		

GOALS: _____

_____

_____

_____

_____

_____

FLOOR ROUTINE	
I DID WELL	MUST WORK ON

BEAM	
I DID WELL	MUST WORK ON

VAULT	
I DID WELL	MUST WORK ON

BARS	
I DID WELL	MUST WORK ON

📅 DATE	📍 MEET LOCATION

GYMNASTIC LEVEL	

	PERSONAL BEST	TODAY'S SCORE
BEAM		
FLOOR		
BARS		
VAULT		
ALL AROUND		

GOALS: _____

_____

_____

_____

_____

FLOOR ROUTINE

I DID WELL	MUST WORK ON

BEAM

I DID WELL	MUST WORK ON

VAULT

I DID WELL	MUST WORK ON

BARS

I DID WELL	MUST WORK ON

📅 DATE	📍 MEET LOCATION

GYMNASTIC LEVEL	

	PERSONAL BEST	TODAY'S SCORE
BEAM		
FLOOR		
BARS		
VAULT		
ALL AROUND		

GOALS: _____
_____
_____
_____
_____
_____

FLOOR ROUTINE

I DID WELL	MUST WORK ON

BEAM

I DID WELL	MUST WORK ON

VAULT

I DID WELL	MUST WORK ON

BARS

I DID WELL	MUST WORK ON

📅 DATE	📍 MEET LOCATION

GYMNASTIC LEVEL	

	PERSONAL BEST	TODAY'S SCORE
BEAM		
FLOOR		
BARS		
VAULT		
ALL AROUND		

GOALS: _____
_____
_____
_____
_____
_____

FLOOR ROUTINE

I DID WELL	MUST WORK ON

BEAM

I DID WELL	MUST WORK ON

VAULT

I DID WELL	MUST WORK ON

BARS

I DID WELL	MUST WORK ON

📅 DATE	📍 MEET LOCATION

GYMNASTIC LEVEL	

	PERSONAL BEST	TODAY'S SCORE
BEAM		
FLOOR		
BARS		
VAULT		
ALL AROUND		

GOALS: _____

_____

_____

_____

_____

FLOOR ROUTINE	
I DID WELL	MUST WORK ON

BEAM	
I DID WELL	MUST WORK ON

VAULT	
I DID WELL	MUST WORK ON

BARS	
I DID WELL	MUST WORK ON

📅 DATE	📍 MEET LOCATION

GYMNASTIC LEVEL	

	PERSONAL BEST	TODAY'S SCORE
BEAM		
FLOOR		
BARS		
VAULT		
ALL AROUND		

GOALS: _____
_____
_____
_____
_____
_____

FLOOR ROUTINE

I DID WELL	MUST WORK ON

BEAM

I DID WELL	MUST WORK ON

VAULT

I DID WELL	MUST WORK ON

BARS

I DID WELL	MUST WORK ON

📅 DATE	📍 MEET LOCATION

GYMNASTIC LEVEL	

	PERSONAL BEST	TODAY'S SCORE
BEAM		
FLOOR		
BARS		
VAULT		
ALL AROUND		

GOALS: _____
_____
_____
_____
_____
_____

FLOOR ROUTINE	
I DID WELL	MUST WORK ON

BEAM	
I DID WELL	MUST WORK ON

VAULT	
I DID WELL	MUST WORK ON

BARS	
I DID WELL	MUST WORK ON

	📅 DATE	📍 MEET LOCATION

GYMNASTIC LEVEL	

	PERSONAL BEST	TODAY'S SCORE
BEAM		
FLOOR		
BARS		
VAULT		
ALL AROUND		

GOALS: _____
_____
_____
_____
_____
_____

FLOOR ROUTINE	
I DID WELL	MUST WORK ON

BEAM	
I DID WELL	MUST WORK ON

VAULT	
I DID WELL	MUST WORK ON

BARS	
I DID WELL	MUST WORK ON

📅 DATE	📍 MEET LOCATION

GYMNASTIC LEVEL	

	PERSONAL BEST	TODAY'S SCORE
BEAM		
FLOOR		
BARS		
VAULT		
ALL AROUND		

GOALS: _____
_____
_____
_____
_____
_____

FLOOR ROUTINE

I DID WELL	MUST WORK ON

BEAM

I DID WELL	MUST WORK ON

VAULT

I DID WELL	MUST WORK ON

BARS

I DID WELL	MUST WORK ON

📅 DATE	📍 MEET LOCATION

GYMNASTIC LEVEL	

	PERSONAL BEST	TODAY'S SCORE
BEAM		
FLOOR		
BARS		
VAULT		
ALL AROUND		

GOALS: _____

_____

_____

_____

_____

FLOOR ROUTINE	
I DID WELL	MUST WORK ON

BEAM	
I DID WELL	MUST WORK ON

VAULT	
I DID WELL	MUST WORK ON

BARS	
I DID WELL	MUST WORK ON

📅 DATE	📍 MEET LOCATION

GYMNASTIC LEVEL	

	PERSONAL BEST	TODAY'S SCORE
BEAM		
FLOOR		
BARS		
VAULT		
ALL AROUND		

GOALS: _____

_____

_____

_____

_____

FLOOR ROUTINE

I DID WELL	MUST WORK ON

BEAM

I DID WELL	MUST WORK ON

VAULT

I DID WELL	MUST WORK ON

BARS

I DID WELL	MUST WORK ON

📅 DATE	📍 MEET LOCATION

GYMNASTIC LEVEL	

	PERSONAL BEST	TODAY'S SCORE
BEAM		
FLOOR		
BARS		
VAULT		
ALL AROUND		

GOALS: _____

_____

_____

_____

_____

_____

FLOOR ROUTINE	
I DID WELL	MUST WORK ON

BEAM	
I DID WELL	MUST WORK ON

VAULT	
I DID WELL	MUST WORK ON

BARS	
I DID WELL	MUST WORK ON

📅 DATE	📍 MEET LOCATION

GYMNASTIC LEVEL	

	PERSONAL BEST	TODAY'S SCORE
BEAM		
FLOOR		
BARS		
VAULT		
ALL AROUND		

GOALS: _____

_____

_____

_____

_____

FLOOR ROUTINE	
I DID WELL	MUST WORK ON

BEAM	
I DID WELL	MUST WORK ON

VAULT	
I DID WELL	MUST WORK ON

BARS	
I DID WELL	MUST WORK ON

📅 DATE	📍 MEET LOCATION

GYMNASTIC LEVEL	

	PERSONAL BEST	TODAY'S SCORE
BEAM		
FLOOR		
BARS		
VAULT		
ALL AROUND		

GOALS: _____

_____

_____

_____

_____

FLOOR ROUTINE

I DID WELL	MUST WORK ON

BEAM

I DID WELL	MUST WORK ON

VAULT

I DID WELL	MUST WORK ON

BARS

I DID WELL	MUST WORK ON

	📅 DATE	📍 MEET LOCATION

GYMNASTIC LEVEL	

	PERSONAL BEST	TODAY'S SCORE
BEAM		
FLOOR		
BARS		
VAULT		
ALL AROUND		

GOALS: _____

_____

_____

_____

_____

_____

FLOOR ROUTINE	
I DID WELL	MUST WORK ON

BEAM	
I DID WELL	MUST WORK ON

VAULT	
I DID WELL	MUST WORK ON

BARS	
I DID WELL	MUST WORK ON

📅 DATE	📍 MEET LOCATION

GYMNASTIC LEVEL	

	PERSONAL BEST	TODAY'S SCORE
BEAM		
FLOOR		
BARS		
VAULT		
ALL AROUND		

GOALS: _____
_____
_____
_____
_____

FLOOR ROUTINE	
I DID WELL	MUST WORK ON

BEAM	
I DID WELL	MUST WORK ON

VAULT	
I DID WELL	MUST WORK ON

BARS	
I DID WELL	MUST WORK ON

📅 DATE	📍 MEET LOCATION

GYMNASTIC LEVEL	

	PERSONAL BEST	TODAY'S SCORE
BEAM		
FLOOR		
BARS		
VAULT		
ALL AROUND		

GOALS: _____

_____

_____

_____

_____

FLOOR ROUTINE

I DID WELL	MUST WORK ON

BEAM

I DID WELL	MUST WORK ON

VAULT

I DID WELL	MUST WORK ON

BARS

I DID WELL	MUST WORK ON

📅 DATE	📍 MEET LOCATION

GYMNASTIC LEVEL	

	PERSONAL BEST	TODAY'S SCORE
BEAM		
FLOOR		
BARS		
VAULT		
ALL AROUND		

GOALS: _____
_____
_____
_____
_____

FLOOR ROUTINE

I DID WELL	MUST WORK ON

BEAM

I DID WELL	MUST WORK ON

VAULT

I DID WELL	MUST WORK ON

BARS

I DID WELL	MUST WORK ON

📅 DATE	📍 MEET LOCATION

GYMNASTIC LEVEL	

	PERSONAL BEST	TODAY'S SCORE
BEAM		
FLOOR		
BARS		
VAULT		
ALL AROUND		

GOALS: _____

_____

_____

_____

_____

FLOOR ROUTINE

I DID WELL	MUST WORK ON

BEAM

I DID WELL	MUST WORK ON

VAULT

I DID WELL	MUST WORK ON

BARS

I DID WELL	MUST WORK ON

🗓 DATE	📍 MEET LOCATION

GYMNASTIC LEVEL	

	PERSONAL BEST	TODAY'S SCORE
BEAM		
FLOOR		
BARS		
VAULT		
ALL AROUND		

GOALS: _____

_____

_____

_____

_____

FLOOR ROUTINE	
I DID WELL	MUST WORK ON

BEAM	
I DID WELL	MUST WORK ON

VAULT	
I DID WELL	MUST WORK ON

BARS	
I DID WELL	MUST WORK ON

	📅 DATE	📍 MEET LOCATION

GYMNASTIC LEVEL	

	PERSONAL BEST	TODAY'S SCORE
BEAM		
FLOOR		
BARS		
VAULT		
ALL AROUND		

GOALS: _____

_____

_____

_____

_____

FLOOR ROUTINE	
I DID WELL	MUST WORK ON

BEAM	
I DID WELL	MUST WORK ON

VAULT	
I DID WELL	MUST WORK ON

BARS	
I DID WELL	MUST WORK ON

	DATE	MEET LOCATION

GYMNASTIC LEVEL	

	PERSONAL BEST	TODAY'S SCORE
BEAM		
FLOOR		
BARS		
VAULT		
ALL AROUND		

GOALS: _____
_____
_____
_____
_____
_____

FLOOR ROUTINE	
I DID WELL	MUST WORK ON

BEAM	
I DID WELL	MUST WORK ON

VAULT	
I DID WELL	MUST WORK ON

BARS	
I DID WELL	MUST WORK ON

🗓 DATE	📍 MEET LOCATION

GYMNASTIC LEVEL	

	PERSONAL BEST	TODAY'S SCORE
BEAM		
FLOOR		
BARS		
VAULT		
ALL AROUND		

GOALS: _____
_____
_____
_____
_____
_____

FLOOR ROUTINE	
I DID WELL	MUST WORK ON

BEAM	
I DID WELL	MUST WORK ON

VAULT	
I DID WELL	MUST WORK ON

BARS	
I DID WELL	MUST WORK ON

	DATE	📅 MEET LOCATION

GYMNASTIC LEVEL	

	PERSONAL BEST	TODAY'S SCORE
BEAM		
FLOOR		
BARS		
VAULT		
ALL AROUND		

GOALS: _____

_____

_____

_____

_____

_____

FLOOR ROUTINE

I DID WELL	MUST WORK ON

BEAM

I DID WELL	MUST WORK ON

VAULT

I DID WELL	MUST WORK ON

BARS

I DID WELL	MUST WORK ON

Made in the USA
Monee, IL
21 March 2023

30329874R00066